Returning to Eden

Rachel Shields

BookLeaf
Publishing

India | USA | UK

Presentation by *BookLeaf Publishing*

Web: www.bookleafpub.com

E-mail: info@bookleafpub.com

ISBN: 9789358734751

First edition 2023

DEDICATION

To those who have encouraged my writing, and
especially to my grandmothers, who always
treasure my work

ACKNOWLEDGEMENT

If it were not for my Savior, Jesus Christ, I would have no words to write. I am thankful for the gift of language and expression. More than that, I am deeply thankful for His precious gift of salvation. To Him be the glory!

PREFACE

The book you are holding is undeniably a
Christian book. The poems composed here, in
some way, all point to the brokenness and
dissatisfaction in this world and the
consummation of the kingdom of Jesus Christ.
Everything around us has fallen under sin's grip,
and we are a long way from the Eden God
created. This world now is full of sin and
sorrow, but for the one who has put their faith
and trust in Jesus, giving their life to Him,
incredible hope breaks through this darkness.
One day, Jesus will return, and He will right all
these terrible wrongs and heal every wound. The
works in this book express my deep longing for
the day when He makes all things new, when I
walk with Him in the garden.

Summer's Death

As the last glimmers of summer die
The trees their joyous leaves shed
The summer of the heart sounds the saddest
goodbye
And hangs its lowly head

Oh how quickly youth is finished
The sweet joys now restrained
The vibrance of life diminished
As love lives now from expression refrained

How bitter does this death encroach
Upon the recesses of the heart
As winter's cold, dead hands approach
To swiftly rend love apart

Drought and Rain

This drought has scorched the earth
Leaving death in its arid path
Burned by the sun's dry and fiery wrath
The ground aches and cries out for rebirth

This once-lush valley now a desert
Grieves for what has been lost
Sin entered and we all bear its cost
All of creation groans under this curse

While a drop here and a drop there
Do not sate this parched and thirsty soul
What a hope these gentle droplets share
That the life-giving rain will come
And make this broken, barren world whole

Smoke

When will the smoke clear
And beauty return?
How long shall we lie in fear
While all around the world burns?

How Long?

When
Will these looming clouds
Open in release
And give birth to rain
To sate the thirsty ground
Until then
These ones that promise
Growth
Life
Shadow the earth
Obstructing the sun's healing rays
How long
Until neither cloud nor parchedness
Oppress any further?
How long, O Lord?

Sleep

Weary bones
Busy head
Weighted mind
Tired bed
Longing for rest
Tangled in depths
Harbored thoughts
Arresting sleep

Darkness Dies

A brilliant sun ablaze
Dressed in flaming orange
Its glory piercing the ashen sky
As its burning beams unfold

The grey breaks
The smoke dampens
And the dusty haze over this fallen world
Dies a little more

-on seeing a glorious sun in a smoky sky

Cotton Candy Skies

My eyes rose to the sky
And I marveled
For I beheld cotton candy skies
So rich and full and delicious
They intoxicated me
I returned my eyes to the ground
And lost myself in the mundane here
And when I looked up again
I saw not cotton candy skies
But where once they reigned in the heavens
Now lay gray wisps of smoke

Darkness and Day

When I look out o'er the silent trees
As I watch them wave, flutter, in the breeze
My heart be not still, raging like seas,
Rippling, furious, as it does please.

The golden fields hide the golden sun
As at long last, its rays from me run.
When the beams do fade, every one,
Then, at that moment, the day is done.

My heart yearns for dark no more but day
But try, try, try, as I might and may,
The dark will only whisper and say,
Wait, I hold you until the first ray.

Death's Grip

My love forever caged in a glass,
Frozen in time for me to feel
The great grief as tears grace my eyes.
My heart hurts with the remembrance
That days past are not yet to come.
Mothers should not be ripped away from their
children,
Leaving them destitute at a young age.
I am that eight-year-old,
Torn and battered by death's hard grip.
My breath freezes as the lump in my throat
hardens.
Nothing is the same, and because of death,
Nothing ever will be.

The Window

The most beautiful of all I know
Lies behind the eyes.
The face that does show
The heart's truest colors.
The eyes open a window
To let the light reveal
The soul's song, quiet and low,
Beating through burning eyes.

The Weary are Welcome

The weary are welcome
In the Father's safe arms
"Cast your burden here!"
The Blessed One calls
"Your need is met
My riches I share
Toil no more
Find rest here"
What love have You, my God?
None on earth compares

Praise

Running through the Valley of the Shadow of
Death
And the shadows are all around me.
Churning, monstrous waves towering over me,
Help me, Abba, help me, Father, help me!
Every second I sit there,
Lonely and wet,
My Savior comforts me,
And my heart feels at rest.
Realizing the shadows are gone,
I'm out of the depths!
Everything I have will praise God!

Out of the Mire

How firmly I cling to this mire
A burning flame of unholy desire
Clasps my heart so strong
This passion for wrong
This penchant for sin
Claims my life without and within

This self-centered greed consumes
Even while death's threat looms
Promising trouble and strife
Not only in this but also the next life
And still I daftly close my ears
Unwilling my condemning fate to hear

Yet while I go my wicked way
The Savior condescends to say
Grace overflows, mine at no cost to me
He shoulders the burden while I go free
The curse of death never stirred my soul
But this gospel promises to render me whole

The scales fall and my eyes see
The crimson stream shed in love for me
Jesus died and His is the victory
Raised to the Father and seated in glory

He casts my sin into eternal depths
I am alive! Alive! A slave I am no more to death

Saved from sin securely I stand
Yet still I war with the inner man
Dead to death and alive to Christ, still I cry
For the sin I think will satisfy
But when tempted to return to that mire
The Holy Dove whispers, "Look higher"

Though the cares of this life heavily weigh
Hope abounds for that coming day
When all around will bow to the King
His renown none will cease to sing
And together, forever into eternity
With my Savior Jesus will I be

The Cross

How heavy dost this cross seem
Which Thou hast called me to bear
How quick am I to complain
And proclaim this weight unfair

Yet when I look to Calvary
And see the pain Thou bore
My feeble heart is strengthened
To journey forward a step more

Knowing that the cross I carry
Carries the life I received
Truly to death I died
When through the cross I believed

So when I think of Thy life
So freely exchanged for mine
'Tis not a burden but a joy
To bear my cross as Thou bore Thine

Why Me

Why me
Is the question
That sends my mind
Rolling
Spinning
Tumbling into distrust
Running from You
Doubting Your goodness

Why not me
Is the question
That sends me back
Humbling
Softening
Reminding me of truth
Running to You
Trusting Your goodness

For You loved me enough
To shoulder my sin
You chose me
And now in gratitude I ask
Not from complaint
Why do I have
This privilege to suffer?
Why me?

Thy Grace

Only strength from above
Sustains my weary step
What grace, O heavenly Dove,
Dost hold my every breath

How miry the path and dark the way
In which Thou dost gently lead me
Yet how brightly shines the Day
I climb forward in hope to see

O Spirit, prepare my sinful heart
To see Thy glorious face
How kind to me Thou art
For I know Thy wondrous grace

The First Advent

Behold, the angels appeared
That quiet and unknown night.
The shepherds quaked and feared
Before the great and shining light.

The angels rang news of a birth
On a clandestine hillside
Of glad tidings to all the earth,
Reaching far and spreading wide.

For on this unexpected day,
A Savior has been born.
"Hear ye, hear ye," the angels say,
"He is Christ the Lord."

Like never before the shepherds yearned
To know their Savior King.
In their hearts joy burned
For the coming of which we sing.

And so in this unforeseen advent,
To the lowliest and highest of men,
Came a man from Heaven sent
To save us from our sin.

Emmanuel, Emmanuel, do not delay
To ransom us from our toil with sin.
Lord, hasten, oh hasten! that glorious day
Of your coming once again.

No Other

Who has trampled death
By bearing its fierce sting
And giving up His breath?
'Twas no other than the King of Kings

Who has defeated sin,
Utterly rescuing the soul
From accusation without and guilt within?
'Twas no other than the Lord of all

Who deserves all praise
Glory and honor to receive,
Whence from the dead He was raised?
'Tis no other than the Prince of Peace

Who is worthy, He alone,
To ascend before the Father, the great I AM,
And to sit down on the throne?
'Tis no other than the slain and risen Lamb

www.ingramcontent.com/pod-product-compliance
Lightning Source LLC
LaVergne TN
LVHW050311210726
843507LV00020B/3049